Copyright 2020 - by Beth Costanzo

Many of the world's most fascinating sea creatures are some of the biggest. Creatures like the shark, whale, and even the manatee inspire wonder in all of us. But having said this, some of the most interesting animals in our seas and oceans are some of the smallest.

In this post, I want to take a close look at a tiny, yet fascinating sea creature. That sea creature is the **seahorse**. While they are extremely small, seahorses are some of the most beautiful and interesting creatures in our oceans. Whether you plan to scuba dive soon or are taking a trip to your local aquarium, here are some fun facts about the seahorse.

The Seahorse: One of the Most Interesting Creatures in Our Planet's Waters

Whenever you are talking about the seahorse, it's natural to talk about its size. The seahorse's size can range from as small as 0.6 inches to 14 inches. The smallest seahorses are very difficult to see if you were swimming or scuba diving. Even the largest seahorses would require you to focus or to swim right next to them.

Seahorses get their name from appearance. Looking at a picture of them, you would quickly notice that their necks are bent and that they have long heads with snouts. You would also see that seahorses have a very distinctive tail. Putting all of these qualities together, many believe that the seahorse looks like a horse underwater.

While we often use the word *seahorse*, it is important to know that there are many different kinds of seahorses. In fact, there are 46 species of small marine fish that are considered part of the seahorse family. Even though these species have minor differences, they have that distinctive seahorse look.

From appearances, let's now talk about where you can find seahorses. Besides your local aquarium, seahorses can be found in many different places around the world. Typically, they like to make their homes in things like coral reefs, mangroves, and seagrass beds. Seahorses have been found in the Pacific Ocean near North America and South America. They have also been spotted in the Atlantic Ocean and even in the Mediterranean Sea. Compared to some other animals, there isn't an exact place where you have a great chance to see seahorses. You'll just need to get into one of these bodies of water and hope for the best.

One of the most fascinating things about seahorses is how they have children. Many other fish and land animals have females handle all parts of the birthing process. These females do everything from carry their babies, deliver them, and care for them after they are born. The seahorse, however, is different.

Male seahorses actually carry the eggs of future seahorses. What happens is that when male and female seahorses are mating, the female seahorse drops up to 1,500 eggs in the male seahorse's pouch. Male seahorses have a pouch on the front-facing side of their tails. After the eggs are deposited, male seahorses carry these eggs between 9 and 45 days. As you can guess, the eggs are held until baby seahorses emerge from them. Once they break through their eggs, the baby seahorses are released into the water. The male seahorses then start the process again, looking for female seahorses so that they can continue mating during the breeding season.

Seahorses eat different kinds of food. They mostly like to feed on things like mysid shrimp and other small crustaceans. But having said this, they will go beyond these animals. Seahorses have been known to eat things like larval fish and other invertebrate animals.

While the seahorse has an interesting diet, the actual process of feeding can be difficult. This is because seahorses aren't the greatest swimmers. Because of this, seahorses tend to anchor their bodies on things like seaweed or coral. When they are anchored, seahorses rely on their tails and long snouts to catch and eat their food.

But when seahorses catch something delicious, their work is not over. Seahorses do not have a stomach, so they have extremely simple digestive systems. Because of this, seahorses need to continuously hunt and eat. It can be exhausting, but the seahorse doesn't have a choice.

Like many other sea animals, seahorses face the threat of extinction. However, it is much more difficult to track whether seahorses are dying from human and natural activities. This is because of their size. That being said, scientists already believe that there are several species of seahorses that have already gone extinct. It is up to all humans to work together to make sure that animals like the seahorse are not totally wiped out from our world's oceans.

Beautiful Creatures

Ultimately, seahorses are beautiful creatures. Whether you see a picture of a seahorse or encounter one when swimming in the Pacific Ocean, you will notice that they are stunning animals. Not only that, but their mating and feeding habits make them extremely unique creatures.

So while most of the attention goes to larger creatures like sharks or whales, I encourage you to pay attention to the seahorse. You won't regret it!

Worksheets

Tracing

Trace the word then rewrite it.

Seahorse

Counting

Count the seahorses then circle the correct answer

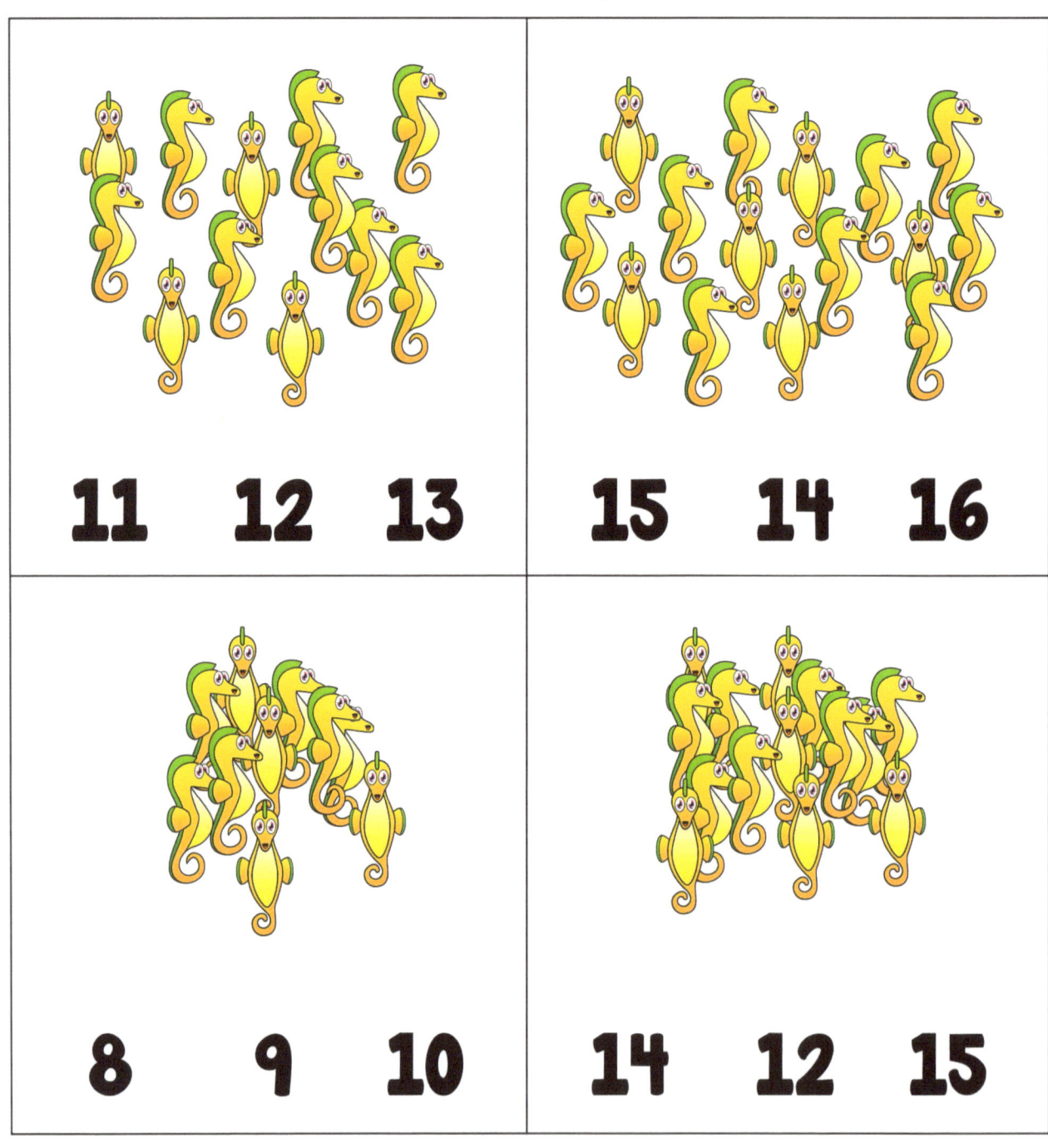

Counting

Count the species then answer in the box

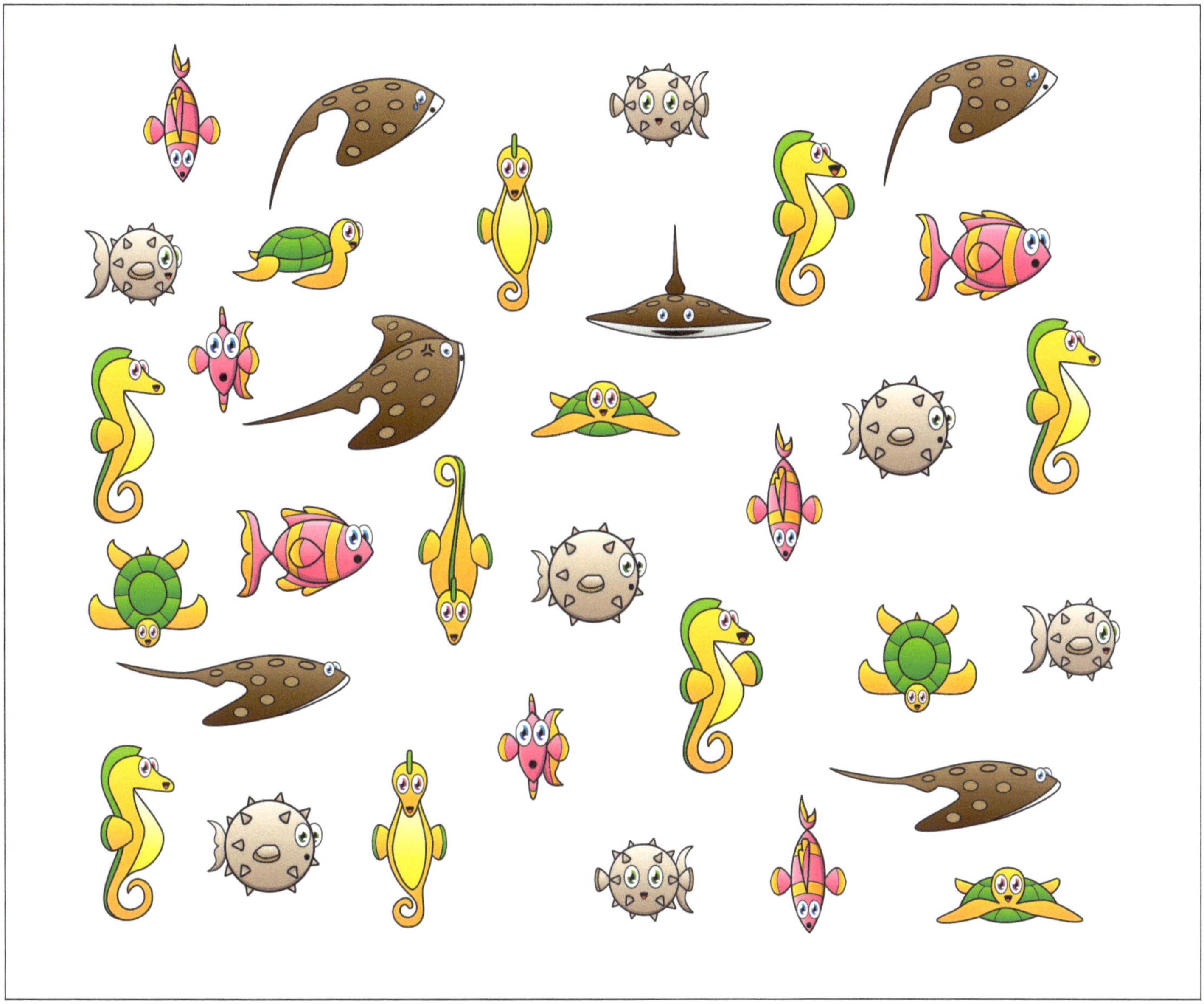

Seahorse's Body Parts

Put the number of each body part of the seahorse in the correct circle

1- Eye

2- Dorsal fin

3- Pectoral fin

4- Coronet

5- Tail

6- Keel

7- Snout

Numbers

Trace Numbers, then cut and paste them in the correct order

| 4 | 6 | 3 | 8 | 10 | 7 | 1 | 5 | 9 | 2 |

Color and decorate the seahorses

Seahorse stick

- Fold the page in the middle
- Cut the seahorse following the lines
- Color and decorate it

- Glue a stick in the interior of the 2 seahorse's sides
- Glue the seahorse's sides

Visit us at:

www.adventuresofscubajack.com

www.ingramcontent.com/pod-product-compliance
Lightning Source LLC
Chambersburg PA
CBHW041437010526
44118CB00002B/97